Moyra Donaldson was born in Newtownards and educated at
Queen's University, Belfast. A pamphlet of her poems, *Kissing
Ghosts*, was published by Lapwing Press in 1995. Two full
collections of her work have been published by Lagan Press,
Snakeskin Stilettos (1998) and *Breaking the Ice* (2001).
Snakeskin Stilettos was reprinted in 2002 by CavanKerry Press,
New Jersey, and shortlisted in America for the ForeWord Book
of the Year Award.

D1354732

By the same author

Poetry
Snakeskin Stilettos
Beneath the Ice

As editor
Down at the Millennium
Alchemy

THE HORSE'S NEST

THE HORSE'S NEST

MOYRA DONALDSON

LAGAN PRESS
BELFAST
2006

Acknowledgements

Versions of some of these poems have appeared in *Poetry Ireland Review*, *Black Mountain Review*, *The SHOp*, *Cuirt Annual*, *West 47*, *Interpoezia*, *Polyphony*, or have been broadcast on BBC Radio 4 and Radio Ulster.

Thanks are due to the ACNI for an Individual Artists Award which enabled me to buy time to work on the collection. Thanks also to Belfast City Council for the Year of the Artist Award which enabled me to work with people from the Belfast Chinese Community.

I would like to thank Martin Mooney for his interest and editorial assistance. Thanks too to those other friends who helped along the way.

'The Phoenix Clinic' was written after seeing the art produced by residents of the Phoenix Clinic in Newtownards, a rehabilitation centre for people with head injury.

'Burial' and 'Signs' were written for the late Maírtín Crawford, much missed friend.

Published by
Lagan Press
1A Bryson Street
Belfast BT5 4ES
e-mail: lagan-press@e-books.org.uk
web: lagan-press.org.uk

ARTS
COUNCIL
of Northern Ireland

ISBN: 1 904652 33 6
Author: Donaldson, Moyra
Title: The Horse's Nest
2006

Design: December
Printed by J.H. Haynes, Sparkford

for John

Take a flat Map a Globe in plano, *and here is East, and there is West, as far asunder as two points can be put: but reduce this flat map to roundnesse, which is the true form, and then East and West touch one another, and all are one ... there is but a step from that to this.*

—John Donne
Sermon 27, preached Easter Sunday, 28th March 1619

Contents

Stubbs at Horkstow

Lord Nelthrope's boy
brings this one to me, not
the usual type, old and broken
but a handsome bay gelding,
still muscled up and fit,
crippled though, tendon
snapped on the hunting field,
no use to his Lordship now,
so kindly donated.

I hold the halter rope,
my assistant cuts the throat,
his knife well practiced
and the keen arc of jugular
blood marking the air
with its hot ferrous smell.
The boy can't watch, pales,
has to be sent indoors
for a drink of water.

The horse goes down neatly,
onto his knees, onto his side,
feet jerking, mixing the mud
and blood into a red paste,
impasto thick: we wait
until he stills and his eyes film,
then the rush to inject veins
and vessels with liquefied tallow
before they collapse.

The tackle is my own design,
an iron bar suspended
by a teagle to which iron hooks

are fixed. Pass these hooks
through the ribs, under the back
bone, fasten them: so the corpse
is lifted, hung, hooves resting
on a plank and I can set them
in the attitude of a horse walking.

It is a long journey
into the body of a horse,
into the structure of reality:
abdomen, five layers
of muscle, peritoneum,
pleura, lungs and bowels,
then the head, stripping
the skin until the muscles
are cleaned and ready
for me to make careful
diagrams, write detailed
explanations, the work
of a day and then another,
on and on, working against
time, the fattening flies,
the smell: I do not flinch.

Ache

When nothing helps,
when the road ahead
can not be measured,

there is nothing to be done
but to keep walking:
one foot after the other ...

Cheyne-Stokes Breathing

I

'Cheyne-Stokes breathing'
the consultant says
and so
I'm left
helpless
again
mother
counting
thirty
sometimes forty
seconds
between
each breath
you take
lifetimes
waiting

and with
each breath
your fear
every time
every minute
fear
for two days
every breath
you grip my hand
a drowning grasp
fierce
you grimace
as if terror is sitting
on your chest

worst of all
I cannot tell
is it life or death
presence or absence
that panics you

after two days
I can't stand it anymore
beg morphine for you
but am refused
four times

until I howl
embarrassing banshee
in the corridor
and they agree
to give you a sedative
at least.

II

Muriel, Joan, Hazel, Elma, Noelene,
John Stewart, Stewart, Lorraine,
Claire, Jannah, John and me,

we are weaving a blanket, stories
for you of you, good memories
to cover you and keep you warm,
to comfort you, and us
as best we can, to still the last
panicked flutter of your hands
with coloured threads of words,

the green hill far away, chalk dust, dun flank
of the cow you'd lay your brow against
as milk flowed, creamy through your fingers,

young men and dance halls, brazen happiness,
red lipstick, flecks of rebellion, caught
against the grey warp of duty, and your faith,

crystal in the weft of time, the bright blue iris
flag of courage—white forget-me-knots
of pleasure in the telling: beautiful as any prayer.

III

My mother is refusing to die
despite the doctor's repeated
'anytime now'
despite the withdrawal of fluids.
For eleven days
my mother eats herself to keep going,
flesh and muscle disappearing,
fed to the unconscious furnace of her will.

At night, when it's just her and me
I tell her everything's already been forgiven,
but as usual she doesn't listen.

Bone and a hank of hair—
my mother is refusing to die.

IV

On the twelfth morning
I keep an appointment
I could cancel
knowing
she'll go
while I'm away
and sure enough

at a quarter to eleven
I feel it happen.

Outside
I turn my eyes
to the sky
in time
to see her disappear
through the space
time continuum
the universe bending
to release her at last.

Not even the faintest
essence of her left.

V

Dear Moyra
I know you have been going through a very
difficult time of loosing your mother,
which I myself am most afraid of and never
prepared for.
I wish you could be peacefully with your
mother in thought of her, now someone
immortal within yourself.
best wishes
Junko

Tollymore

My mother is no ghost
no presence no sign
nowhere

except
beside the Shimna,
where coming back is a counterbalance

to loss—the same paths walked
by generations, the same trees
shading

the paths
although the people
have gone into the flow of time.

June sun illuminates brackish water—
ripples over stone, shadow fish
flicking

their tails against the current.

*

The August forest smells different,
sweeter, decaying towards autumn.
Through the floor's moss and mulch,
fly agarics, yellow fingers of coral fungus.

We know these paths, and the difference:
rowan berries, blackberries, hazelnuts,
chestnuts, all ripening, and underneath
the six swallowed pomegranate seeds.

*

The tail of Hurricane Charley
flicks us two days
and nights of wind and rain,
heavy, incessant rain.
We play cards, drink coffee
and lie awake, listening
to the downpour,

and the Shimna river,
beneath and above the rain,
a great liquid train
of memory,
roaring and rumbling
over rocks, down waterfalls
and out to sea.
We rescue what we can.

Hungry Ghosts

My mother heard ghosts crying,
many ghosts crying
because they were hungry,

her father, mother, sister,
brother, her childhood self:
the little girl who lived

down the lane, in a house
where love never prepared
a table before her.

Me, I sacrifice, light candles,
psychoanalyse: anything
to keep my own ghosts fed.

Monumental Sculptor

When he has cut my mother's name
into the granite, McCormick,
the monumental sculptor,
ESTABLISHED SINCE 1938,
along with the invoice
sends photographs—proof.

Bamboo

Knows how to make use of hollowness,
knows how to be insubstantial,
gives way, sways and bends,
is seldom broken ...

food paper book pipe mast
bucket fence thatch raft
medicine scaffolding
chopstick furniture

The Hummingbird Case

I

Strung up bones of the blue whale,
crystals and fossils and earthquakes;
the hummingbird case, hundreds
of dead hummingbirds, pinned
in attitudes of song and movement,
beaks open, wings outstretched,
fastened forever to a dead tree
in a glass cabinet, turned
wooden legs, decorative carvings
framing their limbo.
I can't take my eyes off it.

*

Bird of superlatives,
smallest warm-blooded creature,
the fastest metabolism,
smallest nest, fastest heartbeat,
fewest feathers of any bird,
best memory of any bird,
remembering how many flowers,
when each was last drunk from.

Bird who can fly right, left,
up and down,
upside down and backwards,
tips of the primary wing feathers
describing a perfect figure of eight
in axial rotation, wings beating

up to seventy times in every second.
The hummingbird alone among the birds,
can hover
in perfectly still air.

                    *

Whitehead and Keates
are the museum's reference,
but they don't know much,
just that the cabinet is walnut
and oak, early 19th Century
probably, probably listed
in the sale catalogue
for Mr. Bullock's Egyptian
Hall, Piccadilly.

A good example,
made purely
as a conversation piece.
A pseudo-natural prop,
(in this case a tree) to set off
the greatest number of objects,
here, around 500 birds,
a guess from the tour guide
who tried to make the count.
The world's smallest bird,
the bee hummer,
is trapped here too.

                    *

Bird from the Left, the spirit land,
messenger between worlds

who knows the secret doors
and passageways: bringer
of smoke to the shaman, tongue
piercer, rain maker, glittering
rainbow fragment, earrings
for Aztec priests, your feathers, held
up to the sunrise at winter solstice,
hasten the rebirth of the stillborn.

II

The parlour maid is a flibberty
—gibbit, so the Colonel's wife
inspects the room herself,
runs her fingers along
the mantelpiece for dust,
adjusts the stems of calla lilies.
A good fire, the silver polished,
candles lit and multiplying
in facets of crystal; the Colonel
needs everything to be perfect.
A year they've been married,
time enough for her to learn
how important it is
to keep the Colonel happy.

She lifts a spoon, and sees herself
distorted by the curve, her pale face,
the darkness beneath her eyes.
She pats her hair, run through
and through with hairpins
to keep its unruliness in check.
The Colonel won't have imperfection.

She sets the spoon down
on the pristine white
starched linen table cloth.
Her nerves are bad today,
she hasn't felt right
since she first set
eyes on that horrible
bird cabinet he bought
last week in Piccadilly.

A real conversation piece—
he said as the men carried
it in, set it beneath the tiger's
head and the elephant tusks.

Last night she dreamt the glass
was broken and the tiny creatures
loose, escaped around her head,
a blur of wings, ruby throats
and stabbing beaks.
She tried to shoosh them away,
flapping her hands, but they flew
into her hair, her eyes, her mouth.

III

THE EGYPTIAN HALL.

Roll up, roll up
to a CORNUCOPIA of wonders and marvels—

We have on display, NAPOLEON'S CARRIAGE
taken at Waterloo: antique marbles, jasper, agate,

vases, tablets, tazzas, superb pictures
of the ANCIENT and MODERN Masters.

NATURAL CURIOSITIES: snakes and crocodiles,
a six legged pig, an ELEPHANT, a RHINOCEROS,

many more strange and wonderful sights
from far off lands and SAVAGE JUNGLES.

Our suggested tour begins with a case of artefacts
from the SANDWICH ISLANDS, many of them

brought back by the celebrated CAPTAIN COOK.
See the wonderful collections of exotic birds

from the AMERICAS and AMAZONIA.
The magnificent plumage of the Bird of Paradise,

tiny jewelled humming birds,
sought out and captured, BROUGHT TO YOU

by that other esteemed explorer of our age,
Mr. HUMBOLDT.

Mr. WILLIAM BULLOCK's amazing collection
formed during seventeen years of arduous research

at a cost of thirty thousand pounds is open to everyone—
ADMISSION ONLY ONE SHILLING.

IV

Yes, ours is a successful business—
taxidermy for the modern scientific age.
We supply the guns and traps and nets
and my son does the traveling, away
for months at a time, sea voyages, Mexico,
Tahiti, The Americas: where explorers go.

He has nimble fingers and he's good at his work:
the peeling and cutting must be done delicately,
not clumsily or the skin may be torn. Taught him
myself: first the back cut from neck to tail, remove
the organs, all the viscera, tongue, trachea, taking
great care to scrape off all the fat, then rub the skin
with a mix of ash, sulphur and alum—that way
they get home to me safe and well preserved.
Lately he's been trying a new recipe, some
French gent's: arsenic in it. You're right,
I'm not one for change for change's sake,
but I'd have to say, the arsenic does a fine job.

I must confess, this last commission's
been a challenge, with my eyesight
not so good and such a number of birds,
hundreds and hundreds—and so tiny,
smaller than the wrens that nest the hedges
round our house, but brighter than wrens,
like little jewels; one small as an insect.
Fiddly to stretch such small scraps of skin
over the artificial bodies; awkward to stuff
with hay, fiddly to stitch: such small skewers
to fix them to the branch, positioning each
bird so that the whole display's in balance.

I think I've got it right, like if I clapped
my hands the lot would just take flight.
I bring an artist's eye to the natural world
even if I say so myself; in years to come,
people will look at this case of birds
and see it as a work of art as much as any
painting or sonnet or sonata, don't you think?
What else is art but the ability to capture life,
pin it down to be admired and wondered at.

V

I know myself
when out of the blue heaven
you plummet before me
a breathless piece of sky
so for a moment I believe
you are the sky
and your bird shape
just light's desire for physicality

you rise and fall with such mastery
how can I not open myself
red petal and nectar: flower for you.

VI

I am the hummingbird the Navajo sent up
to see
what is above the blue sky: that found nothing.

Something and Nothing

... and I am re-begot
Of absence, darkness, death; things which are not.
—John Donne, 'A Nocturnal upon S. Lucy's Day, being the
shortest day'

Wren
    on the windowsill,
         an omen   maybe,
     sends
              my heart flying. I am nothing
if not easy to please:
    then
         the familiar fraction,
    yin of fear
at the heart of every confidence.
           Today
our time is doubly stolen,
           borrowed
    from an overdraft,
      all
      capital depleted:
yet for these hours,
    nothing
is everything,
      a remembered taste
fed mouth   to mouth,
rhythm
on
rhyme,
    like the building of grace,
      curving
and

            I am   in danger,
                dissolving,   loosing
the line
                    becoming
something   else.

Lightning Strike

The calm afterwards holds
a mesmerising light.
We go outside,
into the discharged evening,
the palpable vibration of atoms;
down the shimmering lane,
to look for the glass dagger.

The gorse bush is charred
to its bare bones, the earth still
smolders from the piercing.

Mist rises towards the moon
from the thick drenched grass
of the hayfield, where a black stag
antlered with silver is watching us.

Yourself

Do not give yourself up for a god.
Do not give yourself up for a master.
Do not give yourself up for a parent.
Do not give yourself up for a husband.
Do not give yourself up for a child.

Complaints

I

My lover is the wind,
inconstant, nothing
but change without substance,
hot and cold, whisper, roar
and me the silly
spinning weather vane.

II

My lover is a natural disaster,
earthquake, famine,
a plague of locusts;
I am uninsurable.

III

My lover is a broken reed
and I have nothing to lean on.

Marriage Poem

Secretive again, the evening drifts towards darkness,
the weight of nothing expected—a moth wing brush.
The white freesia, the bamboo blind, the gift horse;
moving between dimensions with the obstinate grace
given to familiar objects and their place in our lives.
What we ignore will never forgive us.

I have left you the torn map and the silence—
will you find me? Will you look in the twilight
where memories drop like bats from the eaves
of the house where we believed, where the garden
grew us and the children conceived us, before the wind
stormed through our hearts and the rains fell?
This is what I can and cannot say—longing never ends,
is the round smooth stone that I hold in my hand.

Love Poem

There is a well beneath our house
but can I call this house
home
when you do not live here
instead choosing some other place
desert where I am a withered tree
and dark winged scavengers perch
and lizards flick their little tongues.
I have counted the grains of sand
and there are too many

you say
you are not my oasis
you are not my love
you are not my quenching

bread is stone
water a mirror
where you watch the blue eye
of the relentless heaven
the hateful mirage of fields
green as jealousy in the rain
and forty days and nights
your heart has been
without water

I say
I am your oasis
I am your love
I am your quenching

come back
to where the well is waiting

Equinox

Too much time
will have passed.
You will wake
in the night to sounds
of anger, weeping,
a dream or not
a dream intruding
through the open
window in your sleep.

You will be stripped
again of everything
you hold yourself
to be, the third time
and the night turning
ugly and without
mediation, the children
lost between
your fingers, slipping
into the sea and no
one to catch them
now except the tides,
the lovers gone
to their own beds,
language drifting
in the air, ashes
of pages taken by
whatever breeze.

You'll close
the window, crawl
back towards
sleep, back
through too much
time, mist that
sunlight can not pierce.

In the Gallery of Sleep

The dream is like a painting:
man on cliff top, the sea
raging beneath.
A fierce wind blowing,
as can be seen by the way
the man is leaning
and the way
the grass is flowing
round his feet.
Rain comes down
in oblique silver streaks.

The dreamer is like a woman
viewing the painting,
providing the narrative.
She is worried either
for the man or for herself,
she's not sure which.
She reaches up,
touches the glass
which is all
that separates her
from the man and the storm.

A Free Lunch

Across the table from this man
who is buying her lunch
she finds herself thinking
of Red Riding Hood
and how the woodcutter
sliced open the wolf's belly
and filled it with stones.
She sees this man
who is buying her lunch
sinking into a river.
She sees his stone-loaded
belly dragging him down.
He looks surprised
as the last of his breath rises
through the water.
She likes this man
who is buying her lunch,
but still, something
about him has brought her
this image of violence,
drowning and stones.

Stone

Know when to be stone.
Regard the ten stone drums
and see that heaven does
not speak, it takes no sides.

Burial

You're in a cold place tonight, little astronaut,
out of reach of Houston, New York, Belfast,
the arms of those who'd hold you back.

Wet red clay that clings to boots,
red planet's heat gone out,
the poet's words unheard,
the spaceship out of sight,
the moon man lost.

Signs

It's tempting to see you
in the blown cherry blossom, petals
that make the doorway read like a haiku.

It's tempting to hear you
in the microphone's crackle of static,
that surges when the poet mentions electricity.

I'm noticing how faces age,
the edges and folds that time insinuates
into features, the shapes that flesh makes.

It's tempting to speculate
that Peter's impromptu gift was really
from you, to say—lighten up for fuck sake.

It's tempting to imagine
the great gulf that death has set
between us, might so easily be bridged.

A Dangerous Woman

i.m. Noelle Vial

Her hands in the washing up bowl, sudsy and warm—
she's a woman who believes in love, miracles
in the kitchen, an angel to trouble the water,
a man to run his fingers across her belly, melding
the edges of where she's been sawn in two,

a woman who believes she can make
something truthful from the soft shape
of a child's throat, a raised fist, a bed
of nettles, a silk blouse; who believes
she can say anything given by air and angels,
by the way a line carves across a white page.

Tongue

I plant the wizened seed of my head
in the winter earth. My tongue stills,
curls back on itself like an old manuscript.
We sleep, the earth and me, all through
the darkest days and dreamless nights
until light begins again and my head
becomes white and tuberous, my green
daughters growing from my eyes,
my tongue a root, sucking nurture
from the death of what was: from
my third eye, a shoot: white flowers.

Tao

One magpie, sorrow
on the monkey puzzle tree
preening its feathers.

Endurance

When you are thrown, accept the fall—
then get back up : keep getting back up.

Dark

The past comes towards me,
arms outstretched, needing
comforted like a small child
who has woken in the dark.

A Local Tragedy

Because I was a small child and impressionable
when my mother told me how they stood
at the door and watched the ambulances go past
I felt I'd been there too,
                                saw the tense faced men,
felt the lashing rain, the wind that would blow you
off your feet it was that strong. I heard the sirens
clanging from Ards past the farm at Drumhirk,
fading on through the Cotton and Ballyvester
to Donaghadee and the Imperial Hotel
where they brought the survivors
and the bodies, the day of the Great Storm,
the day the Princess Victoria sank in the waters
around Mew Island, within sight of shore.

     It happened years before I was born, the story's
     not mine at all: yet I come back to it as if it is.

There was nothing to suggest this crossing
would be different to any other, even with
a storm blowing up as the ship slipped her buoy.

They met the first big sea just past Cairnryan,
waves that smashed the steel doors of the car deck.
A catalogue then of fear and desperation,
mistakes, misinformation, the SOS in Morse
as the radio operator stayed at the transmitter,
the passengers in top deck lounges
and smoking rooms where walls had become
floors when the ship listed onto her beam ends.
Life jackets donned, rafts filled with the women
and children, splintered in the waves, lifeboats

launched from Donaghadee and Portpatrick:
while the sea took its course and the ship rolled over, sank.

This was the sea I paddled in, ankleted by tiny fish;
where wavelets shushed the shore and seaweed
drawn aside, revealed a sideways scuttle of crabs.
Limpets and periwinkles in salty rock pools,
the bloom of sea anemones, harvest of dulce
all the teeming childhood summer—where now
in dreams I saw the drifting faces of the dead,
and heard across sleep the great tenor G
of Mew Island foghorn, sounding mortality.

The bodies washed ashore for days along
the Scottish coast, the Isle of Man, Port Luce, Hango
Hill, Kentraugh, Castletown and Arbory, one hundred
and twenty eight drowned, thirty three survivors.
Reports name only a few, Captain James Ferguson
who went down with his ship, the politicians, Major
Sinclair, Sir Walter Smiles; a handful of the crew.
The others, our 'fellow citizens', aren't singled out

but imagine just one, one woman, or man, or child,
as mouth and nose and lungs fill with the icy cold.

    *

From my bathroom window, every seven seconds
I see the clear white strobe of Mew Island light.
It illuminates the land between me and the sea,
between me and the child I was

a landscape out of ordinary time,
where years slip and reshuffle,
the under layers rising into white

light and dipping beneath again.
Small details and swathes of history:
who knows what will be thrown up
and what is mine?

In Francis Street my grandmother,
recently widowed,
opens her eyes to another day.
Her sister Maggie's there to help
and upstairs, wee Jack is snuggled up
in bed with his five brothers.

Betsy hitches her father's horse
to the block wheel cart to follow her lover,
sets off from the Six Road Ends to meet
death on a battlefield in Ballynahinch.

      Glaciers sweep across, gouging out the crag
           and tail of Scrabo Hill.

      Vikings sail the lough, bury their battle dead
          on the beach at Ballyholme.

      Mrs. McCoubrey's little ginger dog
      barks at me though a hole in the hedge
      as mummy calls me in for tea and bath
          and bed.

      Comgall rises at five am to pray,

   my daddy rises at five am to go to work.

I watch the bones of history settle to dust
and rise again to walk, to speak—
make room for memory of us.

our ordinary extraordinary lives
made up of moments just like this and this and this.

*

'I have been told that his morse code was immaculate
until the very end'
William Broadfoot

Radio Officer Number R 218736,
David Broadfoot, 53,
employee of the Marconi Wireless
Telegraph Company, calmly
amidst the chaos and the noise,
despite the angle of the listing ship,
the pitch and roll, signalled
so that others might live.

At 13.30 hours the order came—
abandon ship. At 13.58
the last message was received
... — — — ...
At 14.00 hours she sank.

*

Of course the ship was not seaworthy:
an enquiry found the owners negligent
on at least two counts..

There are no accidents,
say the bones

and sometimes I hear them
all at once, asking
for remembrance.

*

On Boxing Day TV
I watch a woman run
not away but towards the wave,
towards a cliff of death,
towards her family.

Bangor Girls 1960s

Bangor girls are beautiful and bright and blessed
by tennis courts and ponies, mothers who drive them
to elocution classes and pick them up from parties:
fathers who bring them shoes from Carnaby Street.
The streets they stroll, arm in arm, are leafy, Farnham,
Knockmore, Seacliff, houses guarded by stone lions,
driveways and intricately wrought iron gates, behind
which the Bangor girls do homework, practise scales
and dream of futures bright and beautiful and blessed
as they: they wear their youth around them, as if
naiveté's a charm to keep all evil things at bay.
They will not fade, nor fail, nor falter: they believe.

Water

Water is not afraid,
it plunges over cliffs
and does not hesitate
to go into deep ravines
and places of filth.

In its humility
water always seeks
the lower ground
and so accumulates:
gathers strength
from it's own fall.

Summer of Entanglement

I

House Spider

I hear her feet on the wooden floor,
then at first sight, think it's a mouse,
or my own hallucinatory creature
moving in from the peripheral,
but it's house spider, grown
to monstrous dimensions in the heat
of our comfortable, insulated life.

I call for help and when help
captures her, she fills the whole
circumference of a pint glass
with her huge obscenity, natural,
unnatural: she glares through
the transparent curve between us,
fixing me, sizing me up.

II

Holiday House Spiders

Dots with legs,
hanging,
ready to descend
on their steel ropes,
miniature paratroopers,
fast and brutal

catch and eat

then up again
to the bedroom ceiling.

If I can fall asleep
with them above me
I can cope with anything.

III
Crab Spider ♀

Every time I rinse a cup,
or fill the kettle,
or simply glance out,
I see her, creamy white,
all abdomen and patience,
fattening on the insects
brought to her web by the light
from our kitchen window.

I am entangled:
her single minded spinning,
the delicate angles,
the shape
of her life.

IV
Dream Spider

I wake to find two
fang marks
and a trickle of blood
on my toe.

V
Crab Spider ♂

He turns up late
when summer's

63

nearly over.
Smaller, darker,
quicker than her,
for several nights
he dashes concentric
approaches, jagged
with fear and pheromones
until eventually she has him.

VI
Crab Spider ♀

She's gone, but all around the window's edge
are bulging pearly sacs of spider eggs.

VII
The spider Love

> *... we have bene begotten miraculously,*
> *fostered and geen sucke more straungely ...*
> —from North's translation of Plutarch's *Life of Romulus*

Did you know that cobwebs used to be laid across wounds
to seal them, allow them to heal? Cobwebs against my skin.
They had wrapped me, swaddled me in silk. Bundled me up.
Safe. We lived mostly in the dark, mostly in silence, and I
was happy just to be there, unable to move or see. I felt
their touch on my face as they fed me and I could have
stayed there forever if they had not begun to slowly unwrap
me. I became aware of my body, its fleshiness, compared to
their brittle delicacy. I hoped I could become the same as
them. They comforted me with beauty, spun from their own
bellies. Exquisite angles. They created the alphabet. Without
them you would never have heard this story. They taught
me to make patterns, and although I was slow and clumsy

at first, they were never discouraging. They would bring me more silk. They taught me patience, how to sit and wait. They taught me quickness, how to strike. Living in the rhythm of dust my limbs began to desiccate, as if I was with gratitude becoming one of them.

Girls and Horses

Deconsecrated from the church of the economy,
horses are given over to us, droves of little girls.
We clamber the bone littered killing fields
in mutual rescue, we suck it up, the heady smell
of horse, the horse that sees us when we need
nothing more than to be seen: in our hall
of mirrors he is a way out. We keep our secrets
when we leave the stable, our understanding
of dirt and strength and pain and sweat.
Delicate and powerful, feared and fearful,
girls and horses, one creature.

Miss Mary Anning

It is certainly a wonderful instance of divine favour—that this
poor ignorant girl should be so blessed ...
        —entry in the diary of Lady Harriet Sivester, after visiting
                            Mary Anning in 1824

In my portrait I am staid
and fat and stiff, bonneted,
caped, carrying the tools
of my trade, hammer
and collecting bag,
little dog at my feet,
companion on expeditions
up and down the coast

My father loved to tell
the story of my survival,
the travelling circus,
everyone flocking out
to see the dwarves,
the bearded lady,

then the lightning,
our neighbour falling
blackened to the ground
smoke rising from her head
and me still cradled in her arms.

Father insisted that I
became much livelier
and smarter afterwards,
insisted I'd been marked
out. Some said I'd been
gifted a flash of God-
sight, a vision of an older

Dorset, under-layers,
ancient bones and shapes.
Nonsense. The leap
of imagination was mine
that solved the riddle
of the bones. Ichthyosaurus,
Plesiosaur. The work
was mine, ten years
on each, delicately
uncovering, skillfully
reconstructing

then my name ignored,
what I achieved put down
to the miraculous.

No one can foretell what
life will lay down, stratum
upon stratum, the bones
of self, geology of cancer.
If I am bitter
could I be blamed,
even by my family's
stern dissenting God?

In my portrait I am bland
serene, contented,
bonneted, caped,
my little dog at my feet.

Harvest

Thinking back, the only strange thing
was her wearing her coat night and day,
even when it was warm.

We worked from dawn to dusk
bringing in the winter bedding,
and I kept pace, hefted
the bales against my thigh,
passed them to my father
who was stacking: my hands
were blistered, shoulders sore.

My brother and my mother, back
and forth with the tractor and trailer
to the field, all of us lifting, sweating,
rain forecast, clouds gathering,
the job to be finished.

Later, when the pains tightened
I left the exhausted house
and went back out to the barn.
I made a nest beneath the curved
tin roof and when he was born
I held him, little blue star,
then hid him again, rain on the roof
like the beating of starling wings.

January it was he found it
wedged between two bales
right at the back of the barn.
He laid it out on a bed of straw
then called me to see.
When we asked her, she told us all
but its father's name.
We buried it in the bog field;
that seemed the best thing to do.

Carp

Success never closes
its eyes, never
stops swimming.

The Phoenix Clinic

This is landscape
laid waste,
scorched and cratered,
ash grey, unpeopled and silent.

Where would you look for hope
in such a landscape and yet
these trees, stunted and twisted
still reach their fingers skywards
where one small thread of light comes through

and I am reminded of the gingkoes
less than a mile from ground zero in Hiroshima:
a few months later, budding, bearing leaves.

Elephants

A busy road, a small field,
a corner of my mind—
three elephants
from Circus Vegas
rock gently, shifting
their wonderful weight
from one foot to another,
chewing their cud.

Here's also a great estate,
a crone in a cave
and bones, extinction
hanging from wires, all
antlers, eye sockets
and fleshless nostrils,
in the long winter of ancient
forest, sycamore and oak.

Here's all this and something else
I haven't quite made out.

Notes Towards a February Poem

Pain is waiting in the nerves: the hawk is waiting on the wing.

I do not like this dream,
the house, the rooms where doors open only inwards
and everything is dusty, dark, neglected;
where I am lost.

What do you want from me you whipped dog,
you small cur of grief sitting beside me, always pleading
and always there. Do not go on and on like this.

I have forgotten much more than I remember,
huge tracts of memory, like tundra, bare and featureless.

I am the girl with the beautiful horse, full of grace
in the split second of suspension.

When I am Old

I'll have dewlaps and a hump and say *what* all the time
in a cross voice: on every one of my bony crony fingers,
a ring. My lips painted with a slash of bright fuchsia,
I'll drink margaritas by the tumbler full and if my dealer
dies before I do, I'll just have to look for younger suppliers.
I can't imagine not being interested in sex, but if it happens
so be it, really I could do with a rest, complete hormonelessness.
I may forget who I am and how to find my way home, but be
patient, remember I've always been more than a little confused
and never did have much of a sense of direction. If I'm completely
demented, I'm depending on friends: you know who you are.

Nest

I wake beneath a chestnut tree,
back against bark,
legs stretched out through grass.
Long fingered leaves drip light
and shade haphazardly: the air
is warm. In front of me, a lake
lies like a mirror, and I break
its surface, wash my face
in its salty, ice cold water.

My horse is waiting, shaded and patient,
his skin is comfort, his breath green
as he carries me on his back
to the flat stone altar at the forest's heart.
Being dead, I lay myself down on it
thankfully, and the black bird comes,
lifts me to her round high nest.

Inside the egg,
I am a cell,
dividing and dividing,
first heartbeat,
shell filtered light
warm on my lidless eyes
until time comes
and the shell cracks.

My horse is waiting,
bright and patient:
his skin is sunlight
and his breath air.
Amongst the moss

his bones
are white and dry.

In my beak, I lift
his great rib hull
his long leg bones,
the instrument of his skull,

and in the highest branches
of the tallest tree
in wind tossed waves of leaves,
I build my horse's nest, my ship of bones.